Parks for the People

Parks for the People

A Story about Frederick Law Olmsted

by Julie Dunlap
illustrations by Susan Fair Lieber

A Carolrhoda Creative Minds Book

Carolrhoda Books, Inc./Minneapolis

To my husband, Michael—For all our adventures in parks, great and small

A special thank-you to the staff of the Central Park Conservancy for answering my questions—and restoring the park.

Text copyright © 1994 by Julie Dunlap
Illustrations copyright © 1994 by Susan Fair Lieber
All rights reserved. International copyright secured. No part of this book may be reproduced, stored in a retrieval system, or transmitted in any form or by any means, electronic, mechanical, photocopying, recording, or otherwise, without the prior written permission of Carolrhoda Books, Inc., except for the inclusion of brief quotations in an acknowledged review.

Carolrhoda Books, Inc.
c/o The Lerner Group
241 First Avenue North
Minneapolis, Minnesota 55401

Library of Congress Cataloging-in-Publication Data

Dunlap, Julie.
  Parks for the people : a story about Frederick Law Olmsted / by Julie Dunlap ; illustrations by Susan Fair Lieber.
    p.   cm. — (A Carolrhoda creative minds book)
  Includes bibliographical references.
  ISBN 0-87614-824-0
  1. Olmsted, Frederick Law, 1822–1903—Juvenile literature. 2. Landscape architects—United States—Biography. 3. Parks—United States—History—Juvenile literature.
  [1. Olmsted, Frederick Law, 1822–1903. 2. Landscape architects. 3. Parks.]
  I. Lieber, Susan Fair, ill. II. Title. III. Series.
  SB470.05D86   1994
  712'.092—dc20
  [B]   93-40988
                                                                            CIP
                                                                            AC

Manufactured in the United States of America

1 2 3 4 5 6 – I/MA – 99 98 97 96 95 94

Table of Contents

Introduction

Parks come in all shapes and sizes. Some have just enough room for a few benches or a basketball court. Others, such as New York's Central Park, cover acres with lakes, woods, and meadows. Some city parks, such as those in Boston's "emerald necklace," are linked so people can walk for miles under a canopy of green. And in places like Yosemite National Park, visitors can roam for days in near wilderness.

In the early 1800s, no one could imagine such parks. Most Americans lived on farms or in small towns. Town families often had gardens and barns, and the countryside was just a short walk away. Parks didn't seem necessary.

But America was changing. Cities were growing rapidly, and the new residents often lived in crowded, dirty slums. Rich people could take country vacations, but for the poor, there was no escape.

Frederick Law Olmsted thought cities could—and *must*—be changed. People need cities, he agreed, but cities need parks. Fred designed parks of all kinds, transforming the way our cities and country look and feel.

① Free to Roam

Fred Olmsted sat on the edge of the stagecoach seat, chattering to his father about their trip. How exciting to see the towns and forests of western New York! Fred's father, John Olmsted, smiled at his six-year-old son's restless enthusiasm.

Suddenly, Fred stopped talking. That roar in the distance could only be one thing. Niagara Falls! The moment the stage stopped, Fred scrambled out the door and raced down a wooded path to a rocky overlook. There, he stopped still. Before him a broad, green river swirled around boulders and forested islands until it crashed over the edge of the falls. In the mist churned up by the pounding water, a pale rainbow sparkled. Never would Fred forget that magnificent scene.

Born on April 26, 1822, Fred lived four hundred miles from Niagara Falls in Hartford, Connecticut. Young Fred often walked down the shady streets of the small, thriving city. Among the fine homes, churches, and shops he passed was a store belonging to his father. John Olmsted sold dry goods—mostly cloth and sewing supplies. Profits from the store allowed John to support a large family comfortably.

Fred and three-year-old John Hull Olmsted were the only children from their father's first marriage. Their mother, Charlotte Hull, had died when Fred was only three, and both boys called their stepmother, Mary Ann, "Mother." After their father's second marriage, the family expanded until the boys had six half sisters and brothers—Charlotte, Mary, Bertha, Owen, Ada, and Albert.

John and Mary Ann loved all their children, but with so many little ones they often left Fred to roam on his own. He would shove some crackers into his pockets at daybreak and head down a city street or a dirt road into the country. On his walks, he picked lilies and hunted rabbits along the stone fences. No fox track or woodpecker hole escaped his eyes. His ears heard every hawk cry.

Whenever Fred could not go out exploring, he

found ways to enjoy nature close to home. He pestered an uncle into lending him garden space to grow flowers. An elderly neighbor let the curious boy study his personal museum of butterflies, rocks, and plants. On rainy days, Fred read about the English countryside in his favorite book, *Forest Scenery*. Curled up in his grandfather's attic, he would imagine himself strolling down a sunny English lane.

His parents liked the outdoors almost as much as he did. Whenever John could get away from his store, he would pile the whole family into the carriage. The Olmsteds bounced down rutted roads toward the Connecticut River for a picnic, a swim, or a few hours of berry picking.

John knew Fred loved exploring nature, but he also felt his son needed more serious schooling. A dedicated Congregationalist, John believed that it was Fred's duty to do something for the world— to study hard and learn a useful profession. John regretted his own poor education and dreamed that someday his son would study at Yale College. So he sent Fred to live and study with a nearby parson to prepare.

The parson was also a farmer, and seven-year-old Fred spent more time doing chores than studying.

He gladly helped the parson pick apples and cart them to the cider press that fall. In late winter, he hauled buckets to collect maple sap and tasted hot syrup in the sugaring shack. After washing and shearing sheep in the spring, he helped neighbor boys smoke woodchucks out of their burrows. When the earth warmed in the summer, Fred kicked off his shoes and explored the fields barefoot.

The farm work delighted Fred, but his father was dissatisfied. The Hartford school that Fred went to next also disappointed John. Then he sent Fred to a boarding school. Bullies targeted Fred, the smallest of the sixty boys, for teasing. The teachers also punished the students cruelly. Fred refused to complain, but a classmate wrote Mr. Olmsted that one teacher had pinched Fred's ears until they bled. Furious, Fred's father came to take him home.

Finally, John chose a small school run by Reverend Joab Brace. Nine-year-old Fred and three other boys studied and slept in Reverend Brace's drafty schoolroom. When winter winds whistled through the cracks, the boys huddled around the tiny woodstove to memorize their lessons. Reverend Brace punished every mistake with a sharp rap on the knuckles. A shivering Fred struggled to learn Bible verses and Latin grammar rules, but his mind kept drifting. How he longed to be outdoors!

Sometimes, Fred told stories to cheer up the other students. But Reverend Brace checked to make sure the boys were studying. He took off his shoes before tiptoeing up the wooden stairs to listen at their door. If he heard talking, the Reverend would burst into the room, shouting, "Oh! The depravity of human nature!" Grabbing a broomstick, he beat his students on their shoulders. Fred quickly learned to dodge around Brace's legs and run to the barn, where he burrowed deep into the hay.

For four years, Fred saw his family only briefly on holidays and summer vacations. One summer Sunday, Fred's grandfather found him lying beneath an elm tree, watching its branches swaying in the breeze. Captain Olmsted told Fred about planting the sapling himself as a boy. Nothing in his grandfather's long life as a sea captain had made him as proud as planting that tree.

Too soon for Fred, it was time to go back to Reverend Brace's. School improved a bit in 1835 when his brother John joined him. Always close, the boys became best friends.

When fourteen-year-old Fred returned home that summer, he headed straight for the woods.

Overjoyed to be free from school, he did not notice that he was walking through a patch of a sticky plant called poison sumac. An itchy rash soon covered his arms and face. By the next day, Fred's eyes were nearly swollen shut.

Even a week later, his eyes were still swollen and painful. The family doctor worried that Fred's sight might be permanently damaged. You must rest your eyes, the doctor warned. No more studying!

At first, Fred was thrilled. No more Reverend Brace! Once Fred felt well enough, his father sent him to work as an apprentice to a civil engineer. Learning to make maps and draw imaginary towns was great fun.

But soon his father insisted that it was time for more serious work. Like his father, Fred felt he had a duty to help others. Yet if he couldn't study for a profession at Yale, Fred wondered, what could he do?

②

Restless Spirit

Fred perched on a high stool, scratching columns of numbers with a quill pen. Fred's father had brought him to New York City in 1840 to work at Benkard and Hutton, a French dry-goods importer. There, John hoped, his son would learn how to run a business. Fred tried to like the job to please his father, but he felt trapped in the dull, stuffy office.

Fred cheered up, though, whenever the boss sent him to check in a new shipment at the East River wharves. A forest of masts lined the docks, and flags of ships from all over the world snapped in the breeze. Once Fred found his ship, each bale of cloth for Benkard and Hutton had to be carefully inspected. But his eyes kept wandering to watch the sailors. As the ship rocked gently on its moorings, Fred's heart filled with longing for the sea.

Traffic noise hurt his ears as he walked back to the store. New York's streets were crowded with poor laborers and littered with rotting trash. Life as a city clerk was not for him, Fred decided. Grandfather Olmsted had been a sea captain. Why not go to sea? In spring, a merchant ship would sail from New York Harbor to trade with China. Captain Fox of the *Ronaldson* warned Fred, "We always dislike to take a green hand." But Fred was determined to go.

He packed a sea chest full to the brim with flannel shirts, duck pants, an oil suit, and a remedy for seasickness. On April 23, 1843, Apprentice Seaman Olmsted set sail, three days before his twenty-first birthday.

A few days into the voyage, a gale began to toss the ship. Heavy waves broke across the deck, soaking the crew to the skin. Desperately seasick, Fred crawled into a cramped berth below deck. By the time Fred felt well enough to eat, the fresh food was gone. What remained was a grim diet of salt beef, sea biscuit, and sour gruel. Too weak to climb aloft, he was put to work filing rust off tools.

The *Ronaldson* rounded Africa's Cape of Good Hope and sailed through the Java Sea. In Canton,

China, Captain Fox traded his cargo of ginseng for tea and raw silk. To speed the return voyage, the captain worked his crew harshly. Though sick with scurvy from the poor diet, Fred took his turn trimming the sails, pumping bilge water, and keeping sharp lookout. Later, Fred told his parents, "We were often kept at work with scarce a minute's rest." On one night watch, he fell asleep standing up. When the ship finally docked in New York City, John Olmsted barely recognized his gaunt, pale son.

After his year at sea, Fred wanted to work on dry land. But doing what? Perhaps he should try farming, he thought. To get started, he visited the farms of Connecticut friends and neighbors. Next, he listened in on a few classes on scientific farming at Yale, where his brother John was earning a degree.

To get real farming experience, he became an apprentice at George Geddes's prize-winning farm in New York State. Fred asked George a crop of questions about how to choose the best plants, how to enrich poor soil, and how to drain soggy fields. Fred planted and fertilized and hoed and harvested until his back ached.

His letters home were filled with mouthwatering

lists of the food he was helping to grow—green peas, melons, sweet corn, tomatoes, cherries. Growing food made him feel useful, he wrote. Plus, he could work outside, surrounded by fresh air and beautiful scenery.

Fred's enthusiasm convinced his father to lend him money to buy his own land. Fred's first farm on the Connecticut shore was too rocky to grow much, but in March 1848, he moved to a better farm on the Staten Island coast. From his porch, he could watch ships in New York Bay.

There was little time, though, to enjoy the view. The fields and buildings had been badly neglected. With a large crew of hired hands, he drained wet fields and planted acres of hay, corn, and oats. The fall harvest was bountiful.

At night he sat by the hearth, reading about the latest scientific farming ideas. His favorite magazine was *Horticulturist,* edited by Andrew Jackson Downing. A famous landscape gardener, Downing advised farmers to plant trees, bushes, and flowers around their homes. Landowners, he wrote, should bring nature's beauty up to their doors. Fred felt inspired by his words. As the fire burned to embers, he sketched out plans to beautify his farm.

Fred set a crew to work moving the barns out of sight and building a gracefully curving, tree-lined driveway. To shade the farmhouse, he planted walnut, elm, and mulberry trees. Soon Fred's land looked so much better that neighbors asked his advice about their land. Fred gave it eagerly.

John Hull Olmsted, now a medical student in New York City, spent the weekends with Fred. A nagging cough kept John from helping with chores, so while Fred worked, John talked with a charming seventeen-year-old neighbor, Mary Perkins.

When John and Mary became engaged, Fred was delighted. Another frequent visitor, Fred's father, was just as pleased. One son would soon be a happily married doctor. The other was creating a beautiful, prosperous farm. Their future looked secure.

Despite Fred's love of farming, though, his restlessness returned. In 1850 John Hull announced plans to tour England with a Yale friend, Charles Brace, before getting married. Fred talked his father into sending him along to watch over John's poor health.

Expecting the English countryside he had read about in *Forest Scenery,* Fred was shocked by his first glimpse of England. In Liverpool, coal smoke hung thick in the air. Poor women sat listlessly on tenement porches, while children wearing rags played in the streets. The poverty and pollution were even worse than in New York. Why, he wondered, was city living often so miserable?

Fred, John, and Charles escaped the city to tramp down shady country lanes, their spirits lifting as they smelled the clover. But it disturbed Fred that some of the prettiest places were closed to the public. Many wealthy landowners created woodland gardens, called deer parks, for private hunting. Why should the rich have these parks, he asked himself, while the poor must play in the streets?

One day, the travelers wandered into Birkenhead, a new suburb of Liverpool. The town boasted one of the first parks for the public in England. The park's designer, Joseph Paxton, was a gardener, engineer, and architect. He had needed all his talents to create the rolling park landscape from flat farmland. Hills and valleys had been molded out of the dirt dug to build two lakes, and winding gravel paths had been carved to carry visitors past sweeping lawns and through groves of trees. In the open spaces, city boys played cricket, girls rolled hoops, and toddlers tumbled in the grass. Poor people as well as rich played in the park.

If only New York City had a public park like this, Fred thought, where poor laborers could play and breathe clean air. "I have seen nothing in America so fine," Fred declared.

In his diary, Fred wrote about Birkenhead's "People's Garden" and the problems he saw in England. Once home again, he decided to turn his journal into a book. *Walks and Talks of an American Farmer in England,* published in 1852, impressed critics. Andrew Jackson Downing praised the book as "fresh and honest." Although few copies were sold, Fred had a new direction. He could do more to solve America's problems as a writer than as a farmer.

A newspaper editor who liked Fred's book asked him to write about the biggest problem in 1850s America: slavery. In December 1852, Fred began a four-month journey throughout the South. From plantation after plantation, Fred mailed north detailed descriptions of crude cabins, meager food, and whippings suffered by slaves. But to Fred, the owners' worst cruelty was depriving black people of freedom. Even under the kindest masters, he wrote, slaves suffer in "mind and soul."

Fred's articles in the *New York Daily Times* opened many readers' eyes to the realities of slavery. To convince more people, he began writing books about his Southern travels. The first, *Journey in the Seaboard Slave States,* won Fred acclaim from reviewers (Northern reviewers—many Southern critics called the book unfair). Like his earlier book, though, it did not sell many copies.

Fred's spirits sank. No matter how hard he worked, he could not support himself as a writer. His neglected farm no longer interested him, and he gave it to the newlyweds, John and Mary. Then he borrowed more money from his father to become a partner in a publishing firm. But the company went bankrupt.

At thirty-five, Fred worried that even his patient father thought he was a failure. And his family was not around to comfort him. John Olmsted had taken John Hull, Mary, and their children to Europe in the frantic hope of healing his son's tuberculosis. To Fred, the future had never looked so bleak.

Green Island
in the City

In August 1857, Fred retreated to a Connecticut seaside inn to finish his latest book. Lonely and discouraged, he was glad to meet an old friend, Charles Elliott. Charles was one of eleven commissioners working to set up a brand-new park in New York City.

New York had grown enormously since Fred's days as a dry-goods clerk. Thousands of immigrants and poor laborers lived in cramped slums. The only places New Yorkers could rest or play outdoors were a few neighborhood squares or cemeteries. Some New Yorkers had been campaigning for years for a large public park like England's Birkenhead. Andrew Jackson Downing and newspaper editor William Cullen Bryant had led the pack, and Fred's writings had added another voice calling for city parks.

Not everyone wanted a park, though. Some businessmen thought it would cost too much and take up land that could be used for buildings. But the park idea had become popular with voters. In 1856 the city had bought 778 acres for a park in the center of Manhattan Island. (Developers did not want this rocky, swampy land anyway.)

The Central Park Commission hired an engineer, Egbert Viele, to begin planning and construction. As Charles Elliott told Fred, the engineer needed a superintendent to oversee workers clearing the grounds. Impressed by Fred's farming experience and love of parks, Charles encouraged him to apply for the job.

Fred knew he would have to work hard to get hired. The commissioners, he thought, would wonder whether a sailor-turned-farmer-turned-writer would have the skills to manage rough labor gangs. With a petition in hand, he searched New York City for friends to recommend him. Many people admired Fred's books and were happy to sign. It was the signature of Washington Irving—the famous author of "The Legend of Sleepy Hollow"—that persuaded the commissioners to hire him.

Park Engineer Viele still doubted Fred's abilities.

On a hot September afternoon, Superintendent Olmsted arrived at their first meeting dressed in his finest suit. Viele looked coldly at his new assistant. Calling in a coatless laborer wearing heavy boots, Viele put the worker in charge of Fred. He was led to the messiest parts of the park, slogging through swamps that poor farmers had used for pigsties and slaughterhouses. "The stench was sickening," Fred later complained. Standing knee-deep in black slime, he could hardly imagine a worse place for a park.

The park laborers laughed when they saw their mud-spattered new boss. Most of the men had been given their jobs as favors from politicians who wanted their votes. They did their work— tearing down fences, removing trash, and rounding up goats left by former residents—slowly and carelessly. No one seemed worried that the young superintendent would make them work harder.

Fred was determined to surprise them all. The laborers needed discipline. So he set up strict rules: each man had to arrive on time, obey orders, and not stop work without permission. Crew foremen watched each worker's behavior closely and reported daily to Fred. Anyone who wouldn't follow his rules was fired.

Soon, on daily walks to inspect the park, Fred found crews grubbing out tree stumps, carting stones, burning brush, or yanking out poison ivy. Each crew foreman nodded respectfully to Mr. Olmsted as he passed.

Fred loved his job. He later wrote, "If a fairy had shaped it for me, it couldn't have fit me better." But his salary was small. He had to borrow money for a horse and do without a warm hat. And every day, he anxiously awaited the mail, hoping for word from his brother. John was now in France, still battling his tuberculosis.

Finally, a letter arrived. "Dear dear Fred," John wrote. "It appears we are not to see one another any more—I have not many days, the Dr says." He reminded Fred of their happy times together, writing, "I never have known a better friendship than ours has been." His last request to Fred was to watch over his wife. "Don't let Mary suffer while you are alive." A few days later, John died quietly with his father and wife at his side.

Fred tried to hide from his grief by working harder. The park commission had announced a contest for the final park design, but he was too busy to think of entering. One day, though, a young architect came to ask for Fred's help.

Calvert Vaux had designed houses for country estates created by Andrew Jackson Downing. Fred knew the park land better than anyone, Calvert said. Would Fred help him design an entry? The tiny but forceful man talked Fred into trying. (The $2,000 prize helped convince him too.)

At night after work, the men explored the grounds and discussed their ideas. Both tried to think like sculptors. How could they shape this barren place into a beautiful, useful park? Calvert pictured the park as a masterpiece of country scenery. Fred imagined a country refuge—where poor and rich could escape the city's noise, dirt, and hectic pace.

Olmsted and Vaux began spending evenings bent over Calvert's drafting table, sketching ideas until their fingers ached. Sometimes, their throats ached as well from arguing over which ideas to put in and which to leave out. Later, no one was quite sure who had designed which parts.

Slowly, their ideas and sketches turned into a plan. The sights and sounds of the city, they decided, should be blocked by a thick border of trees. Four roads through the park should be sunk below ground level to protect visitors from city traffic. In the north, sweeping green meadows would let city people stroll through peaceful countryside.

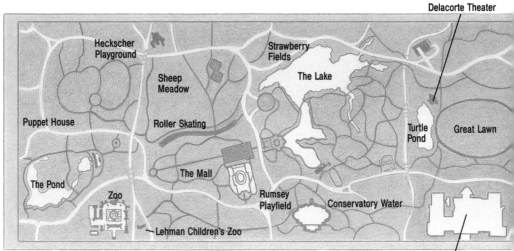

Fred and Calvert's plan for Central Park

Central Park as it looks today

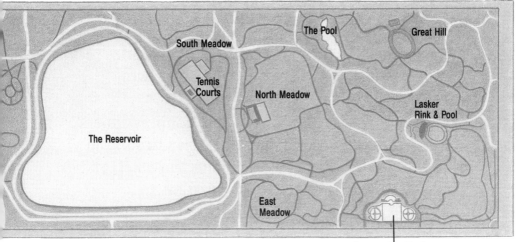

Conservatory Garden

A dense woods on a rugged southern hillside would give them a wilder place to ramble. Nearby would be a cricket field, a space for concerts, and a lake for boating in summer and skating in winter.

The contest deadline approached. Fred and Calvert quickly drew "before" and "after" sketches, showing how the grounds would change. (Calvert probably did most of the drawing—Fred wasn't that good at it.) They worked feverishly on a long report that described their ideas, listed plants to use, and tallied construction costs. Friends who dropped by were even asked to help by drawing grass into the twelve-foot-long park plan. The partners refined their entry up until the contest's final minutes.

On April 1, 1858, they submitted their plan— "Greensward"—the last of thirty-three entries received. Four long weeks later, plan #33 won first prize.

Fred and Calvert rejoiced. The commissioners were so pleased with the plan that they fired Engineer Viele, promoted Fred to architect-in-chief, and hired Calvert as architectural assistant.

Fred disliked his job title, though. He thought of "architects" as people who design buildings. But he was not a "landscape gardener" either.

Planting trees and flowers was just part of the art and science of making a park. Fred and Calvert knew they were helping invent a new profession. They decided to call themselves "landscape architects," meaning designers of outdoor places for public use and enjoyment.

This was just the work he had been looking for, Fred thought. And John Olmsted, reading letters about his son's happiness and accomplishments, breathed a sigh of relief.

Park construction began in earnest. Engineers laid miles of pipes to drain swamp water into the newly dug lake. Explosions echoed as crews blasted out the sunken roads. Three thousand laborers—gardeners, road builders, blacksmiths, carpenters, wagon drivers, stone breakers—worked under Fred's authority to shape the park.

In the midst of construction, Fred thought about future park visitors. Since few Americans had ever been to a park, Fred thought people might not know how to act. So he posted signs telling visitors:

Not to walk upon the grass; (except for the Commons);
Not to pick any flowers, leaves, twigs, fruits or nuts;

Not to deface, scratch, or mark the seats
  or other constructions;
Not to annoy the birds.

And he trained twenty-four men, called park keepers, to teach and enforce the rules. Each day, the gray-suited park keepers practiced patrolling the paths, awaiting visitors.

Though drained by his park duties, Fred kept his promise to look after John Hull's family. Mary had moved the children (John Charles, Charlotte, and Owen) to New York City, and Fred visited them often.

Friends for years, Fred and Mary decided to get married in 1859. The new family moved into an apartment near Fred's office, and Fred began worrying about how to support a family of five.

Money troubles loomed at the park as well. Construction costs were higher than the planners expected. One worried commissioner, Andrew Green, became park accountant to watch expenses. Andrew, though honest and hardworking, distrusted everyone. To cut costs, he reduced wages and fired laborers—yet ordered foremen to finish jobs faster. He decided that one office was using too many pencils and refused to buy more. Getting enough money to do his job became a daily struggle for Fred. He suffered from headaches and lack of sleep.

But Fred's spirits soared in June 1860 when his first son, John Theodore, was born. Eight weeks later, he took his wife and baby out for a drive. Suddenly, their horse bolted, tipping the carriage. The family was flung to the pavement. Mary and John were unhurt, but Fred's shattered thighbone pierced his pants. The doctor predicted that Fred, already weak from overwork, would die within a week. As Fred fought for his life, baby John fell ill and died. Sorrow added to Fred's pain.

Somehow, Fred found strength to recover. While his leg mended, Mary drove him through the park to check on his crews. Andrew Green's power had grown during Fred's two-month absence. Andrew expected exact lists of every expense, yet he would not hire workers to keep the accounts. Fred had to check with Andrew before making any decisions; he could not even have the grass mowed or a bridge repaired without his approval. Andrew's penny-pinching, Fred feared, would damage the park.

By the winter of 1861, Fred could hobble around the park on crutches. One evening, he visited the skating pond, already a popular gathering spot. Inching along the icy path, he felt proud of what he saw. Hundreds of New Yorkers, rich and poor, were enjoying the frozen lake. Skaters glided past snow-whitened trees planted by Fred's crews, and onlookers viewed a scene of natural beauty he and Calvert had only imagined a few years ago.

New Yorkers were becoming quite proud of their new park. It was changing their lives and how they looked at their city. And people in other cities were watching the Central Park experiment. Did their cities need parks? Would this new idea of public places to rest and play catch on? Fred hoped so.

There was work left to finish on Central Park, Fred knew. Piles of stone still littered the ground, and some fields had not yet been planted. But the bitter fights over money were sapping Fred's energy. He was worried, too, about the growing anger between Northerners and Southerners over slavery. What would happen if the nation broke into civil war? Fred loved building Central Park. He told Calvert, "It occupied my whole heart." But perhaps the time was coming, he thought, to move on.

Too Wonderful to Be Believed

When the Civil War erupted in 1861, Fred was thirty-eight years old with a bad leg and poor health. He could not enlist in the Union army, but he still wanted to serve his country. A friend, Henry Bellows, was president of the U.S. Sanitary Commission. The commission was in charge of making conditions as healthy as possible for Union soldiers. Henry admired how Fred had organized Central Park's huge workforce, and he asked Fred to run the commission's office in Washington, D.C.

Leaving Calvert to finish Central Park (and fight with Andrew Green), Fred moved his family to the Union capital. For two years, he took charge of improving the sanitary conditions of army camps and operating hospital ships to care for the wounded.

Fred's efficient sanitary programs strengthened his reputation as an organizer. In 1863 he was offered a job managing the Mariposa gold mines in California. Two hundred miles east of San Francisco, the Mariposa had seven mines, four mills for crushing ore, a railroad, and almost seventy square miles of land. As Mariposa's manager, Fred would make ten thousand dollars a year in gold—four times his government salary. Exhausted by the war, still in debt to his father, and supporting a growing family, Fred took the job. If the mines were rich, his family could follow him west for a frontier adventure.

A cloud of red dust swirled around Fred's carriage on the long road to Mariposa. To Fred, the parched, almost treeless plain he crossed looked dead. He finally reached Mariposa headquarters in Bear Valley at nightfall. The rocky main street, lined with shabby stores, inns, and saloons, looked gloomy in the fading light.

For the next five weeks, Fred rode through Mariposa studying the estate. Some mines and mills looked abandoned. Machines needed repairs, and timbers bracing the tunnels were crumbling. Chances for a rich strike did not look good.

But one day, Fred climbed down a mine shaft to

inspect the veins of ore. Knocking off a chunk of quartz, he held a candle up to the rock. Flecks of gold glittered in the flickering light.

Fred wrote to Mary, urging her to bring the children. But his letter also warned, "You must be prepared for a very hard life." Their only neighbors would be miners—men who wore guns to breakfast. In Fred's first three days, a store was robbed and two men were stabbed. But the weather was the worst news. September temperatures soared to 110°F, and the wind "seems to come out of an oven."

While waiting for his family to make the long journey, Fred worked to improve the estate. He ordered construction of a new mill and repairs of mine tunnels and machines. Geologists were sent searching for new veins of gold. The mills needed more water power to crush the rock, so Fred drew plans to build a canal. Concerned about the miners, he lowered prices at the company stores, planned a reading room, and invited a doctor to move to Mariposa.

Most of the changes cost money, and the mines were not yet producing enough gold to pay for them. So he cut the miners' wages to lower costs— and the miners rebelled by striking for two weeks.

Troubled but still optimistic, Fred pinned his hopes on a new mine that experts said would be rich.

The family, including Fred's two-year-old daughter, Marion, arrived with the spring rains. Home was a roomy apartment over a company store. Bear Valley had no school, so the children were free to roam the Sierra Nevada foothills. Fred often rode beside them on his bay, Dash, teaching them names of flowers and trees. Watching his children riding burros over hills of wildflowers, Fred grew fonder of the California landscape.

Summer heat drove the family out of Mariposa to visit Yosemite Valley, a two-day ride east in the cool mountains. The Olmsteds had read early explorers' descriptions of Yosemite's natural wonders. Leaving dust-choked Bear Valley behind, the hot travelers were refreshed by the tangy scent of a mountain pine forest. Though anxious to reach Yosemite, they could not resist stopping to camp near the giant sequoias in the Mariposa Big Tree Grove. Fred and twelve-year-old John Charles tried to stretch their arms around the ancient cinnamon-colored trunks. Fred told Mary that these were the grandest trees he had ever seen.

On August 13, 1864, the trail brought the family to Inspiration Point overlooking Yosemite Valley.

Nothing Fred had read prepared him for its beauty. Granite cliffs nearly a mile high loomed over a broad green valley dotted with trees. Following the trail into the valley, he found waterfalls, higher and more delicate than Niagara, cascading down the steep walls. Even the jagged, overhanging cliffs looked peaceful behind a soft, white haze. In his notebook, Fred called Yosemite "too wonderful to be believed."

After three weeks in the valley, Fred returned to bad luck in Mariposa. The new mine yielded much less gold than the experts had predicted. Fred's optimism faded.

He was glad to have another, more exciting task to think about. On September 28, 1864, the California governor announced the appointment of Frederick Law Olmsted, respected designer of Central Park, as head of the new Yosemite Commission. The commission would oversee the creation of a state park in Yosemite Valley and the Mariposa Big Tree Grove.

Fred inspected the struggling mines by day and worked late into the night on his plans for Yosemite. He could imagine a time when millions of people would visit the valley from all over the country—and the world. Building roads, shops, hotels, and restaurants for the tourists would destroy the scenery Fred called "the greatest glory of nature." Unlike the Central Park site, he believed, the Yosemite landscape should not be changed. The valley's beauty would inspire visitors more than anything a park designer could create. Somehow, the park must preserve the natural grandeur while still allowing people to experience it.

Fred wrote a long report explaining these ideas to the other commissioners. Roads in the valley should be limited, he argued, to one narrow carriage lane winding through the trees. Instead of fancy hotels, there should be cabins and campsites with only "simple necessities." It is the duty of government, he wrote, to protect Yosemite for people today—and forever.

While Fred was finishing his report in 1865, a San Francisco bank threatened to take the Mariposa property to pay the estate's debts. The only solution Fred saw was to lease the mines to another mining company. But once the new managers took over, Fred would be out of a job.

Heartsick and homesick, Fred was cheered by letters from his old partner, Calvert Vaux. Since Fred had left New York, Calvert had struggled to complete Central Park, including sixty-five acres added in 1863. Fights with Andrew Green had finally forced Calvert to leave the park, but he wanted to return. Fred should come back, Calvert wrote, and help protect their creation. With New York's booming economy, at least they wouldn't have to fight over money.

Letter after letter urged Fred to rejoin their partnership. The triumph of Central Park had won Calvert and Fred national—even international—fame. Since the Civil War had ended in April 1865, Calvert thought cities all over the country would now want parks designed for them. Calvert reminded Fred that he was an artist. Designing beautiful landscapes was what God meant for him. If Fred returned to New York, Calvert wrote, "We may have some fun together yet."

If he left California, Fred worried, what would happen to Yosemite? But then he thought about Central Park. "I love it all through," he wrote Calvert. "There is no other place in the world that is as much home to me." He had made enough money to repay his debts to his father. He could now afford to return to the work he loved.

(5)

Park Keeping

On clear fall Sundays in 1865, visitors streamed into Central Park. High-tailed horses pulled in carriages driven by men wearing top hats. Ladies trotted in riding sidesaddle. Couples on foot pushed baby carriages or strolled arm in arm. And children wearing moth-eaten mufflers raced inside to jump in piles of golden leaves.

Forty-three-year-old Fred may have felt like running and leaping too. Calvert had convinced the park commissioners to rehire the partners as Central Park's landscape architects. Fred had a fresh chance to make sure the park lived up to his dreams.

As weeks passed, though, he realized that Central Park had problems. Almost everyone seemed to want park space for a favorite activity. Baseball players wanted ball fields, carriage drivers wanted racetracks, and museum-goers wanted museums.

The partners opposed the changes, fearing damage to the park's natural scenery.

People pushed especially hard for a zoo. A temporary menagerie in the park already housed deer, bald eagles, cockatoos, monkeys, and Cape buffaloes. Pressured by the commission, Fred and Calvert finally agreed to design a zoo. But they insisted it be constructed on land outside the park. To them, keeping the park beautiful was as important as building it.

But protecting Central Park was not their only job. Just as Calvert had predicted, city people all over the country now wanted parks like New York City's. Many wanted to improve city living, as Fred had hoped. Brooklyn, Albany, Philadelphia, Chicago, and San Francisco asked for advice or park plans. Other clients requested landscape plans for college campuses and hospital grounds.

One of the partners visited each new job site, getting to know the land and how it would be used. After developing a general plan, the partners hired engineers, architects, gardeners, and draftsmen to help work out details and draw final plans. The office of "Olmsted, Vaux & Company," at 110 Broadway, became the busiest landscape architectural company in the nation.

OLMSTED, VAUX & COMPANY

110 BROADWAY

The Olmsteds lived on Staten Island, a short ferry ride from the Brooklyn park project. In June 1866, Fred's father arrived for a visit. One day he toured the Brooklyn park with Fred. How proud John felt of the beautiful way his son helped others!

But soon after his father's visit, Fred got bad news from California. Some of Yosemite's commissioners now fought against spending state money to protect the valley. Fred's ideas about how to stop damage by tourists were being ignored. Hotels, roads, cattle, and fences already scarred the valley's scenery. Fred was furious—but too far away to do anything about it.

He also had more troubles in New York. As the city grew, more people were proposing changes to Central Park. Fred realized that New York needed parks all over the city, with lots of room for many different activities. And, he believed, the parks should be connected by broad, tree-lined roads. The roads, which Fred called "parkways," could bring natural scenery and fresh air deep into the city. Instead of being separate islands surrounded by city, the parks would tie the city together.

But there was not much land left in New York City. And most of the city planners thought of parks as decorations—pretty, but not as important as offices and factories. Fred and Calvert wrote reports and drew plans to change their minds. A few parks and parkways were built, but most of New York's last acres were soon built over.

Still determined, Fred looked for another place to try out the partners' ideas. In August 1868, he visited Buffalo, New York, to study possible park sites. From the carriage, Fred could see that Buffalo still had lots of land without buildings. But it was growing fast. People moved there every day to start new jobs. Many assumed that Buffalo, like other cities, was doomed to ugliness.

But Fred saw a solution. City growth, he said, should be planned around open spaces. Instead of picking one park site, Fred proposed three parks connected by parkways. Then Buffalo, he predicted, would not feel cramped like other big cities. And Buffalo's citizens would never feel too far from nature. The city planners were convinced. When Fred returned home, he and Calvert set to work designing Buffalo's new park system.

It was a great success from the start. No one had believed a city could be so pleasant.

On one of his many trips to Buffalo in 1869, Fred decided to visit nearby Niagara Falls. Seeing the falls he loved as a child, Fred felt sick. The

Niagara River's once-wild shores were crammed with trinket shops, cheap hotels, and advertising signs. Landowners charged fees for a peek at the falls. Tourism, which Fred feared would damage Yosemite, was destroying Niagara Falls. He was too far away to protect Yosemite, but Fred promised himself he would fight for Niagara Falls.

Right now, however, Central Park took all of his attention. In 1869 a group of politicians known as Tammany Hall took control of the New York City government. Tammany Hall thought the park should show off the city's wealth and achievements—not give people a place to enjoy nature.

The park became a huge construction site. Thousands of workers were hired in exchange for their votes. They stripped branches off trees, smoothed rough ground, and replaced native plants with flower beds. Plans were drawn for a conservatory, an opera house, a fancy zoo (Fred and Calvert's had not been built), and other grand buildings.

Tammany's new, poorly trained park keepers failed to enforce park rules. Park scenery suffered, as vandals stole plants and broke equipment. Visitors had to dodge speeding carriages and put up with noise and litter.

Fred and Calvert were horrified. But the new

commissioners would not meet with them to hear their complaints. In November 1870, both were asked to leave.

Fred's only happiness that year came from his family. At forty-eight, he was overjoyed to have a new son. Fred was determined that young Henry would someday follow in his footsteps as a landscape architect. A few years later, he even changed the boy's name to Frederick Law Olmsted, Jr.

In 1871 the *New York Times* published evidence that Tammany Hall politicians were stealing millions of city dollars. The scandal rocked New York, tossing Tammany out of power. Andrew Green was appointed city accountant to clear up the money mess, and Fred and Calvert were rehired to repair Central Park.

Once again, the partners worked side by side on their park. But there was tension between them. Articles in newspapers and magazines often gave Fred most of the credit for the park's design. Calvert was jealous and blamed Fred, while Fred thought he had always treated Calvert fairly. In October 1872, Fred and Calvert agreed to end their partnership. Although both stayed on as Central Park's designers, Fred took on more of the responsibilities for maintaining the park.

Three months later, Fred was at work when a telegram arrived, asking him to rush to Hartford. He reached home in time to say good-bye to his dying father. Fred wrote to a friend, "A kinder father never lived."

Fred could not stop working to mourn. Tammany Hall was regaining strength. He raced to repair the scenery and retrain the park keepers, but each year the city gave him less money. By 1877 Tammany politicians controlled the park board. To get rid of Fred, the board proclaimed that the park was complete. On January 5, 1878, over twenty years after his arrival, Fred was kicked out of Central Park.

Dozens of Fred's friends protested the firing in New York's newspapers. Though Calvert was not dismissed, many doubted that he could protect the park alone. Fred, his health broken from work and worry, followed doctor's orders to take a long vacation.

⑥
Painting with Lakes and Trees

The roar of Niagara Falls rang in Fred's ears. He was exploring a lushly forested island between the American and Canadian sides of the Niagara River. Linked to the New York side by only a footbridge, Goat Island had not been ruined by construction, as the riverbanks had.

For years, a few Americans and Canadians had voiced outrage at the eyesores built around Niagara Falls. European visitors had criticized North Americans for destroying their greatest treasure.

At last in 1878, Canada's governor-general invited New York State to help create an international park. This was a startlingly new idea. New York governor Lucius Robinson liked it and asked Fred and surveyor James Gardner to write a report on the condition of the falls. From Goat Island, Fred and James realized how much damage had been done.

Their report, submitted in 1880, described a view of "solid ugliness." The riverbanks were lined with "mills, carpenter shops, stables, 'bazaars,' icehouses, laundries with clothes hanging out to dry, bath houses, [and] large, glaring white hotels." Clearly, there was little left of the falls' natural scenery to preserve.

The solution, Fred and James proposed, was to restore the land—an exciting new approach. They wrote that the state should purchase a mile-long strip along the New York shore above the falls, plus the still-wild islands in the river. Buildings should be demolished and the grounds replanted with native wildflowers, bushes, and trees. Nothing artificial—stores, statues, flower beds—should be allowed.

Just like Fred's Yosemite report, the Niagara report argued that the government had a duty to protect natural treasures for all people, not just a few "money-getters." Not everyone in New York agreed. Shop and hotel owners along the river objected loudly to losing their businesses. The state's new governor insisted that seeing Niagara Falls was a luxury, so why should taxpayers pay for a park?

Niagara's defenders realized that people needed to learn more about the park idea. Fred and James began a publicity campaign, urging everyone they knew to write letters and newspaper articles about saving Niagara. Restoring the falls would be a long battle, but Fred vowed to stick with it.

Of course, it was not his only project. Besides building Mount Royal Park in Montreal, Canada, he was landscaping the grounds of the U.S. Capitol and drawing plans for several important parks in Boston. He worked in the neat first-floor office of his family's New York City brownstone. Next to Fred sat his stepson, John Charles, carefully practicing the drafting skills Fred was teaching him.

In 1883 chances for restoring Niagara improved. A new governor, Grover Cleveland, backed the idea of a state park, or reservation, there. Now only the state legislators had to be convinced!

It would take all the public pressure Fred and the other park supporters could rally. They formed a new group, called the Niagara Falls Association, which blanketed the state with articles, petitions, and pamphlets. New Yorkers responded by wiring and writing the legislature, demanding that a park be created.

The legislators authorized the buying of the land in a bill signed by Governor Cleveland on April 30, 1883. But who would design the park? Fred waited impatiently for the politicians to decide.

That spring, the Olmsteds bought a new home closer to Fred's Boston work. The rambling farmhouse was in Brookline—a countrylike suburb only a short trolley ride from the city. Naming the place Fairsted, Fred enlarged the house and turned the yard into a miniature park.

Work kept piling up, including designs for the campus at Stanford University and George Vanderbilt's Biltmore estate. And there were always old projects to finish or fix. To keep up, Fred worked with other designers and draftsmen. He also took on a new partner—John Charles. More rooms were added to Fairsted to make office space for everyone.

With all the work, Fred needed well-trained assistants. No schools yet taught landscape architecture, so Fred designed a training program for apprentices. Students were required to take tough university courses in architecture, horticulture, engineering, and drawing. He assigned stacks of books to read and plans to copy. But the students' favorite part of training was following Fred around a park site. Watching their teacher study the plants, soil, and shape of the land, they learned how he worked with nature to make each park unique.

Fred advised each student to keep learning on his own and to become a "professor to yourself."

Finally, in 1886, Fred and his former partner, Calvert Vaux, were asked to design the Niagara State Reservation. The aging artists worked together once again to restore the natural area around the falls. Their design was applauded worldwide. When Canada dedicated its Niagara park in 1888, the dream of an international nature preserve became a reality. Thousands had contributed to this triumph. But without Fred, said one Niagara park campaigner, "there would be no State Reservation at Niagara today."

At the same time, the Boston parks were taking shape. Fred told his partners, "Nothing else compares in importance to us with the Boston work." Their creations included several neighborhood parks scattered through the most crowded parts of the city. Their design for a system of five parks linked by parkways won national fame. These connected parks, known as the "emerald necklace," would eventually be seen by many as Fred's masterpiece. Fred predicted that their Boston work would do as much to promote city planning as Central Park had done to inspire the creation of city parks.

Fred never stopped fighting to protect his first park. In 1892 Tammany Hall politicians and some wealthy horse owners pushed for the construction of a seventy-foot-wide racetrack in Central Park. Calling the track "unjust and immoral," Fred helped raise a public outcry. The track was canceled. To Fred, the victory was sweet.

Also sweet were the honors and praise showered on the balding, gray-bearded man for his dedication and achievements. In 1893, seventy-one-year-old Fred was delighted by two scholarly awards. The boy who never attended college had grown up to receive honorary Doctor of Letters degrees from Harvard and Yale on the same day. Each award recognized Fred for leading the nation in bringing the beauties of nature into city life and preserving the country's natural treasures.

Fred valued the tributes of friends and artists most. Famed architect Daniel Burnham called him an artist who "paints with lakes and wooded slopes; with lawns and banks and forest-covered hills; with mountainsides and ocean views." Perhaps his most cherished honor was a friend's book on trees, dedicated to "Frederick Law Olmsted, the great artist whose love for Nature has been a priceless benefit to his fellow-countrymen."

Afterword

After almost forty years devoted to creating parks, illness and trouble with his memory forced Fred to retire. He passed his last five years at McLean Hospital in Massachusetts, on grounds he had designed years before. Fred died on August 28, 1903, with Frederick Law Olmsted, Jr., at his side.

Fred's sons carried his name and ideas into the twentieth century. From their office at Fairsted, the Olmsted brothers created parks, park systems, suburban communities, and plans for cities throughout the nation. Landscape architecture became a respected profession.

Over the years, many of Fred's parks have been neglected or destroyed. But individuals and groups are struggling to protect and restore some of his designs. The Central Park Conservancy is dedicated to restoring the Greensward plan and keeping it alive. New York City schoolchildren now help with replanting and cleanup of their beloved park.

An environmentalist before the word was invented, Frederick Law Olmsted believed that people learn to love nature only as long as there are natural places left to enjoy. His parks are living monuments to his ideas.

Important Parks

Designed by Frederick Law Olmsted
That You Can Visit

Beardsley Park—Bridgeport, Connecticut

Belle Isle Park—Detroit, Michigan

Central Park—New York City, New York

Cherokee Park—Louisville, Kentucky

Franklin Park—Boston, Massachusetts

Jackson Park—Chicago, Illinois

Lake Park—Milwaukee, Wisconsin

Niagara Falls Reservation—Niagara, New York

Mount Royal Park—Montreal, Quebec

Riverside Park—New York City, New York

South Park—Buffalo, New York

Prospect Park—Brooklyn, New York

Bibliography
of Major Sources

Primary Sources

Olmsted, Frederick Law. *The Cotton Kingdom.* New York: Alfred Knopf, 1962.

———. *Public Parks and the Enlargement of Towns.* New York: Arno Press, 1970.

———. *Walks and Talks of an American Farmer in England.* Ann Arbor: University of Michigan Press, 1967.

Olmsted, Frederick Law, Jr., and Theodora Kimball, eds. *Forty Years of Landscape Architecture.* New York: Putnam's Sons, 1928.

The Papers of Frederick Law Olmsted, Vols. I–V. Eds. Charles McLaughlin and Charles Beveridge. Baltimore: Johns Hopkins University Press, 1977–1990.

Secondary Sources

Roper, Laura Wood. *FLO: A Biography of Frederick Law Olmsted.* Baltimore: Johns Hopkins University Press, 1973.

Rosenzweig, Roy, and Elizabeth Blackmar. *The Park and the People: A History of Central Park.* Ithaca, NY: Cornell University Press, 1992.

Runte, Alfred. "Beyond the Spectacular: The Niagara Falls Preservation Campaign." *New York Historical Society Quarterly* 57 (1973): 30–50.

Zaitzevsky, Cynthia. *Frederick Law Olmsted and the Boston Park System.* Cambridge, MA: Belknap Press, 1982.